Chronicles of PAIN

Leaving the Pain of the Past Behind

To Yedit

Blessing

[signature]

Chronicles of PAIN

Leaving the Pain of the Past Behind

SHARON BLAKE

Hunter Heart Publishing
Colorado Springs, Colorado

Chronicles of Pain: Leaving the Pain of the Past Behind
Copyright © 2014 by Sharon Blake
First Edition: December 2014

All definitions were taken out of Webster's online dictionary, WordReference.com.

To order products, or for any other correspondence:

Hunter Heart Publishing
4164 Austin Bluffs Parkway, Suite 214
Colorado Springs, Colorado 80918
www.hunterheartpublishing.com
Tel. (253) 906-2160 – Fax: (719) 528-6359
E-mail: publisher@hunterheartpublishing.com
Or reach us on the internet: www.hunterheartpublishing.com

"Offering God's Heart to a Dying World"

This book and all other Hunter Heart Publishing™, Eagles Wings Press™ and Hunter Heart Kids™ books are available at Christian bookstores and distributors worldwide.

Chief Editor: Gord Dormer
Book cover design: Phil Coles Independent Design
Layout & logos: Exousia Marketing Group
www.exousiamg.com

ISBN: 978-1-937741-78-5
Printed in the United States of America.

IN MEMORY OF

Margaret Duncan,
My Grandmother

"You always wanted our family to come together and I want you to know that we are working on it!"

ACKNOWLEDGMENTS

To my real Father, the Most High God, my Redeemer, my Deliverer, my Restorer – All the thanksgiving and praise belongs to You. You saw me before I was born and knew Your plans for me, plans for good and not for evil. Thank You for not giving up on me. Thank You for Your mercy and grace. Thank You for Your love and faithfulness.

To my beloved children, I love you all. I extend my deepest, sincerest apologies for ever hurting any one of you.

To Karen Wells, Chris Croft, and Sue Turner – Thank you so much for your guidance. This journey to recovery became easier because of you.

To my pastors Joe and Pamela Bowman – I praise God for both of you. Your transparency and being real helped me become more honest with myself.

To Pastor Wendy Treat, when I was just beginning my recovery, I went to your weekly Word Shops, and the words you spoke I know came straight from God to help keep me sober.

To everyone who taught me to believe that love was an impossibility and that pain was my destiny, thanks to all of you. I wouldn't have found love had I not looked for it, and wouldn't have looked for it if I already had it.

(Poem)

Transcribe the feelings I have inside, place them neatly on a piece of paper, to unfold what I have to say, to tell the story that was once a painful state in which I chose to live and play.

Transcribe this way of life to see clearly the thoughts of life. Can you transcribe for me the beauty of things to be when they are ugly, cold, and grey? (Sigh) When at its worst, I feel like death is on its way…

Transcribe those feelings for me, make it plain and clear. Help me see and understand your plan when I clearly do not know what you are doing or which way I should go. Can you help me on this road? Maybe it's not for me to know, maybe it's supposed to unfold before my very eyes as I get into this thing called life, as I show up every morning suited up and ready to go. It's like a canvas painting that unfolds with each stroke; like music as you place your fingers on the keyboard and the melody begins to unwrap itself; like this poem, this spoken word …

Transcribe for me the story of life and what it is all about. Transcribe for me the ups when I am feeling so high and the downs when I am all burnt out.

Can you transcribe those moments when I feel so deep and dark inside, when I can't get up, and when I can't move around...when lifting my head is too much to think about ... uuuuggghh!!!

Transcribe this painful state called my life.

TABLE OF CONTENTS

INTRODUCTION

This book is my journey to recovery. It is a story of pain and hurt, of joy and healing. It is a testimony of a prostitute, a liar, an alcoholic, and a drug addict. It is an experience of a child who grew up without love, or rather a wrong concept of love, and growing up seeking for that love. It is a life lived seeking for love, getting hurt, and hurting others in effect.

This book is a story of my experiences and how I remember my childhood/life to be. I decided to write this book as a way to deal with my pain, but then soon learned that my pain was just not "my pain". It deserved a voice, in order to help someone else.

My purpose for this book is that someone would read it and know that they too can come out of pain, and that they too are capable of love and being loved.

To everyone who has caused me pain, I forgive you. I did not write this book to condemn, but to shed light on dark places, in order for healing to occur.

My deepest desire is that someone, anyone, find God in and through their pain.

I started to write this story on October 4, 2010. I was just beginning in my recovery and all I knew was that I was in hell and someone sold me an illusion of why I should reside there.

Join me as I recount my journey.

Chapter 1

HOME

We loved to play outside and we loved to hide in the yard, but when darkness began to settle, we knew we would have to go in.

Here is where my story begins.

I have a question before we start. What was your childhood's fondest memory about? I'll tell you mine, if you tell me yours. The memories that followed me into adulthood seemed to be a perfectly calculated scheme; one that I thought I would surely die of. But not before a trip to Hell where I resided and I thought I was doing well? What a concept, you see, to live in a state of insanity. What's even worse is not knowing that you are the one who doesn't know it ... not knowing the perfectly woven web of life's game. This is what I went through. I think it's time to let you know how I came out. Will you go with me on a journey to my past, in order to recover all that was lost?

So, my fondest memory and the main thing that comes to my mind when I think about my childhood is this ... LOVE WAS PAIN! This was what love meant to me.

I was about seven or eight; I don't quite remember the date, but I do remember my step-dad coming home and awakening me. He told me to get up and clean the kitchen, and I had better get it done right away. He made it very clear that no one was to help me. As he went to the room, I remember bowing my head (it's as if I can see it clearly) and began crying, because I knew I would have to put the dishes away and I could not reach the cupboards to get them there. He knew it and I knew it too! So I cried as I dried that coffee cup, I knew what was going to come. After a while, my mom came out of the room and she looked at me with sadness in her eyes. She gave me the stepstool to put the dishes away. As she was leaving the kitchen, she turned to me and smiled with sadness in her eyes. That was the last time I remember my mother ever showing me love as a child. The abuse we endured as children was constant and we thought it was just life.

The next morning I woke up and my step-dad was all messed up; he was mad and angry as usual. He called my name and I knew it was my turn again to get it, and get it good was what I got. I went into the kitchen and he asked who helped me put the dishes away. I put my head down. He looked at my mom and said, "I know you helped her B----!" He dragged her into the room and as usual, all we heard was "Stop, stop!" After he was done with her, it was my time to receive yet another beating. I knew it was coming, so I cried and waited outside and a beating was what I got. My sisters got one too and he said it was my fault, that if it wasn't for me, they wouldn't have received a beating that day.

I was the darkest one in my family and in those days, the darkest had to pay! We got punished almost every night and day. Our lives were stressful, and the environment we lived in was stress-filled. I was mostly singled out, because of the color of my skin (but they said it shouldn't bother me anymore and that I should just ignore it; so I did). I remember him telling me all the time that I would definitely do most of the hardest work, because of the color of my skin. I did end up doing the hardest work. I scrubbed his precious wooden chairs with a toothbrush, inch by inch; it took all day!!! But he did promise me that I could go out and play when it was done, since he knew it would be dark before I was finished. I was so happy at the thought of being able to go outside that I didn't pay attention to his devilish quirky smile. This was a common practice with him, that we would get rewarded for doing something demeaning. He would make us strip butt naked and then beat us like animals, as he smiled with anger. I remember him smiling with anger a lot, as he enjoyed our pain and teaching us to endure it! His bouts of anger and punishments could last for hours upon hours at a time. All the while my mother was in ruin. Wasn't she? Could she have stopped all this? But why? "Why?" I asked myself that question all the time as a child. All I knew is that I wanted my mom to get us out of this house!!!

My step-dad would love to go on these tyrants and very long lectures; we would have to sit at the table many nights and listen to them. It would be so late, but we had better not fall asleep while he was talking, or we would get beat! He would call them "rap sessions," (as if we had a say) but we knew it was our time to get beat up and talked to all night long. This happened every time he came home drunk. I can remember taking naps when I knew he was going to go drinking, just so I could stay up at the table at night. I wanted to show him that I could endure all that he wanted us to. I didn't want to make him mad anymore; I just wanted him to like me and be his favorite, even though I knew he hated me. I thought that if I could make him like me even a little, just maybe we wouldn't get a beating that day. He made sure I knew that the darkest of the bunch had to endure. I was always told because I was the darkest, I would have to accept what I got and not expect more, because dark people got the least and that was just the way it was going to be. These words rang in my head every rap session we had. I started to feel so ugly and bad that I became even angrier. I had to endure his entire wrath. I was the last one excused from the table and was always the one to stay awake for these late night raps. I did what I was told and never talked back! Moreover, he still never really liked me, but for some reason, I kept trying. I didn't want to get beat up anymore, so I would do whatever I had to do so as not to endure that pain of being whipped again. He beat us with whatever he felt he wanted to use on that day – a belt, an extension cord, or a switch that I had to go get myself. I hated being whipped. I hated it! Indeed, I never wanted any man to hit me. So I had to do what I had to do, and that was to endure the verbal and physical abuse. I remember saying "Let him say what he wants and don't make one frowning face, and just maybe he won't hit us today."

I think he started to like me when I listened to him and didn't fight him with a frown on my face. I would smile at him as he tore me down; I would smile at him when he said I was too dark and that when I grew up, I better be glad to have any man that wanted me, because I was ugly. "No one likes dark-skinned people" (keep in mind, I was chocolate, but the rest of my family was high yellow) was all I heard every day and every night! I had to do whatever people asked of me. I had to fit in, because I was dark-skinned. Whatever I was asked to do I had to do, because no man would truly ever want me, unless I endured.

Our childhood experiences taught us that a man and his wife would fight and that if you were the child, your job was to clean and then you get to eat. Quite simple, it seemed. From the outside, at least, we looked like one happy family. But what went on behind closed doors was another thing.

The one thing that mother did do was take us to church! I loved the singing at church. My sisters both could sing; they were sopranos you see. But me, I was only an alto. So church is where I learned to 'let go' through singing. I wanted nothing more than to sing a song. My mom taught us to obey all the religious laws, but forgot the most important thing, and that was LOVE. I think, to be fair, maybe what she showed us was what she knew of Love? The Bible says, "Train up a child in the way they should go and when they are old they won't depart." Well, we were trained alright. We were trained to know that love is pain and that's how it goes. Hmmm… what do you mean? Well this is how we were trained.

- You stay with a man that abuses you and your kids.
- You endure the pain of a whipping.
- You stay with that man, even if he hurts you and your kids.
- You take verbal abuse, because you have to.
- No one will want me because I'm dark, so I had to accept anything and anyone just to be a part of something.
- Verbal abuse is normal communication, that's just how you talk.
- Physical abuse was a normal part of life (especially when you argued, went in the room and then came out smiling).
- This is what love is and this is how you keep a man.

I wanted my mommy to get us out of this house and away from him. The last real horrible memory I have of him was when he beat my sister so bad. All we knew was that she was gone and she didn't come back for a while. But when she did, she was never the same as she was before.

Abuse in any form should not be tolerated this is what I do know. I was not taught this as a child. We must be very careful what we, as parents, teach and allow our children to experience. WE ARE RESPONSIBLE FOR WHAT WE TEACH OUR CHILDREN. THEY WILL GROW UP TO LIVE AS THEY HAVE SEEN US DO.

Chapter 2

THE MOVE

When we moved I thought, "Wow, finally we will get away from this man!" I was so happy, but he followed us and stayed for a brief while. It really didn't matter anymore, because the damage was already done. The feelings of disgrace of who I was and the feelings of 'wanting to be wanted' overwhelmed me. I wanted someone to just love me! See, my mom was preoccupied with keeping him (for whatever her reasons may have been). I don't know!

From ugly to uglier ... we moved from a place called (literally) White Center to the Central District. I have to tell you that

White Center was a neighborhood in West Seattle that was predominantly white. We were the only black family that lived in the neighborhood. We moved to a predominantly black community (how confusing for us).

In White Center, our house was constantly being toilet papered and we woke up to the writings of KKK in red spray paint on our bright yellow house. We knew that many white folks didn't like us, but a few did and those were the ones we played with. We had to constantly watch our backs, which was why we stuck together as sisters, and no one was going to kick our butts! We were constantly on guard, because we didn't know if the next door neighbor, the one who smiled at us, was the same person who sprayed KKK on our house. See, we learned that it didn't matter if white people said that they liked you. Underneath all that, they could very well hate your guts! We were taught not to trust most white men.

One thing I can say was that we learned from some white people how it was to be a phony! We experienced those teachers who would be nice to you in front of others, but when you were alone, they would really let you know how they felt! We knew in school that we were second best, because that's how we were treated. Our wonderful public school system let us know that we were different and we would not get the same treatment as the rest of the other kids that were white. No, you didn't have to tell us we were less. You treated us that way and then expected us to grow up balanced! No, we were far from balanced. We were confused, scared little girls who could not and would not trust anyone! Not even our own mother.

As children, we learned that we had to fight for everything and not to trust anyone. These were the nutrients that were placed in our soil for us to grow in. We go from living in a predominantly white neighborhood, to an all black neighborhood. Wow! What a way to confuse a child. When we lived in White Center, we learned to talk as the white folks did. We were too proper for black folks. So, not only were we not accepted by white folks; I found out that we weren't accepted by black folks either. My hair was long and pretty, but it was feathered like the white girls in our old neighborhood, we wore "Nordy's" from Nordstrom and our pants were pulled up too high. So here we go again, the need to fit in was what I had to do, in order to endure what was going to come soon. Trying to be accepted and constantly being rejected seemed to be the theme of my young life, rejections were what I knew. Always being 'almost good enough' seemed to be me.

I met a boy in this new neighborhood! He went to our church and he used to always want me to play with him on the stairs when no one was there. He kissed me and touched me in places that felt really good. I knew I liked what he was doing, but I was too scared to go all the way. But I would never give it up to him, so eventually; he started not to like me. I really wanted his attention. I realized that he had others on his mind and that made me really sad. I hated to feel like he didn't want me! All I know was after that, I really just wanted to be accepted by men and boys.

So, I became a tomboy. I played basketball religiously with all the boys everyday outside the church. And that is where I met a boy who wanted more from me and this time, I was not going to let him go! I will do whatever it takes, because the pain of rejection was too hard to take! He lived right across the street from me, so when we were done playing basketball, we had to walk the same way home. I thought he really liked me, because we would play basketball together. I loved to play basketball; see, it kept me from thinking about home. And I was good at it too.

The boys used to want me on their team, and I loved the attention. I thought the attention he was giving me was real and I never realized that we didn't spend any time outside of us playing basketball. But that was enough for me, since I was getting some attention again. I would take what I could get and that would be fine, at least he was playing with me. Then one day, when my mom was gone, he wanted to kiss me and then he wanted to go all the way, but I was scared and all I knew was that I didn't want what happened to me with the boy at church to happen to me again. So I gave him what he wanted, I had sex for the very first time. I was only a teenager, but I can remember my step-dad's words that no one would ever want me, because I was too dark and I would have to do whatever a man wanted in order to keep him, so I did. I can remember when it happened. I felt so alone after we did it. I was like, "Is that all; are we done?" It was my first time and it was not special at all. I do not remember feeling anything special after that. He never really wanted anything else to do with me, except in the case of the possibility of getting some more. But I didn't really like what I felt, so I didn't want to do it anymore (so, what you won't do the next girl will). He met another girl that gave it up all the time and that was it for me and him. I used to walk home and hold my head down when I would see him and his other girl sitting on his stairs. I remember watching him laugh with her and talk with her, and I wondered what was wrong with me!

I went to the doctor. I was tired all the time and my mom kept asking me what was wrong. She took me and we found out I was pregnant. What's that all about? I only had sex once, this could not be true. I was devastated and I didn't know what to do. All I wanted was for people to accept me, I wanted to fit in. But what I got was pregnancy and in that day and age being a teenage mother was unacceptable. Now I was really being rejected, especially by society. I remember the look on my mother's face, one of disgust and disgrace. She really never looked at me that I can remember. I know she would always look past me, but this time she looked me dead in my eyes and let me know how she really felt. Oh wow, I got her attention. Finally, she will show love towards me.

Here I am fourteen and pregnant, and don't even know what happened. I never got to enjoy the very act of having sex. I mean really, God! My baby was born, I named her Vashon. She was so beautiful, so pretty; the best thing that ever happened to me. I loved her and she needed me to take care of her. The only thing about this was I didn't know what I was doing with a baby. I had just finished middle school. I felt bad, because I didn't know what to do with her and eventually, as time passed, my mother began to take on the bulk of the responsibility of caring for her. But my mom didn't want too much to do with me. I think maybe she was embarrassed of me, because of our church status. Well that was how I felt back then. I went to all my doctor's appointments by myself and people used to look at me and stare. Women would look at me with a surprise 'oooh weee' she is pregnant, poor thing. I felt alone most of the time. I was pregnant and no one wanted anything to do with a pregnant girl. Whatever remaining thought I had of ever getting a boyfriend was gone.

I lived in a house with my mother and two sisters and I felt so alone. I never really did anything one on one with my mom. We never really bonded ever as a mother and daughter. Our relationship was more of her providing for us and guiding us down the path she thought was right. I believed that I was the one child that, for some reason, she disliked! I am sure getting pregnant didn't help either. So I looked to my baby's grandmother and from some of the people in the church for help. They would tell me how to do things, simple things that I didn't know, because I was so young. I was in that church, but I was so full of pain and anger. I wanted to belong to something so bad, but it seemed as though I could never get it! I loved to sing; singing made me feel like I was somewhere else. But the only problem with that was I wasn't confident enough to sing, so I stayed in the shadows of everyone else. I was slowly starting to want to get away from all the rejection and I wanted someone to want me! I was starting to feel like I couldn't breathe! I felt like if I didn't get someone or something to like or accept me, I was just going to die! I wanted to run away from this life that I knew. I wasn't really thinking about anything else, but I had this uncontrollable urge to get away. But I had a child, so I tried to learn how to be a mom.

My daughter's grandmother showed me how to do things for my daughter, but I never really felt like I was doing things right. My mom had my daughter most of the time, because I was at alternative school trying to get my GED. I didn't know how to be a mother! Let's face it Sharon. My mom seemed to really love my daughter a lot, it was as if she loved and wanted her more than she wanted me. I was going to learn how to be good and I set out on a journey to do just that. I just wanted to fit in some-where, anywhere. So I began to hang out with the wrong crowd. I got a taste of drinking and smoking weed and I liked it...a lot ...well, at least the drinking. Before I could get really out of hand, I started to go to church at a different church from the one my mom took us to. The youth ministry there was good. I loved it! I started to get close to two women there and they truly cared about how I felt and what I was going through. They wanted to know how they could help me and it was wonderful. One problem though. My mom didn't want me to spend so much time with them. "Ugh! For real, I am at church, for real? How, why, what's the problem? I don't freaking understand this at all!" I kept going and I learned that God was really real and the Holy Spirit was real and Jesus loved me. Huh? I thought church was what you did, and you only went because your mom made you and it was the right thing to do. But to have a real understanding that Jesus really loved me was a new concept. My God-mom taught me so much and I loved her more than she will probably ever know. She took me under her wing and taught me every-thing. She showed me how to pray and how to see God in every way. I wished she was my mom at times, but I still loved my mom. It's just that I couldn't ever seem to do anything right in her eyes. I was heading down the wrong path, but now I am going to church, at a good church with good people (or so I thought) and now, me going to church was too much?

I remember wanting to go to a church event one evening and my mom simply did not want me to go at all; it meant so much to me. I cried and called my God- mom and she talked her into it. My mom didn't like the fact that I called her. It was as if she had to do what was right, because someone else knew she was wrong. So she had to do what was right at that time, and she resented me for that. She was a Christian?

I grew up to believe that they were not really nice people, because of how she treated me. I always felt judged and I could never do anything that was right, and that was very frustrating. How dare she think that I wasn't good enough for her if I was pregnant, or that I am going to church? What was I supposed to do? So I just ignored her and kept going to church, until the people in the church showed me that they, too, could be just as cold (with the exception, my God-mom). I wound up leaving that church, because I was so hurt! They had hurt me too! Okay, I guess that is what is supposed to happen? But I was only a teenager. What was I supposed to do with all this pain? The women that had been placed in my life to help me or show me any kind of love kept getting ripped away from me. I was alone again, but this is what love is right? Love is pain (Oh yeah it is. Remember Sharon, you only get what you get and you better accept it, because you are lucky to get anything at all!)

My God-mom was also hurt in the process, so it was hard for her to help me anymore. I was alone again, but this time I had learned the feeling of how it felt to be with people who actually wanted you to be around. I wanted that more than anything in the world. So, that's just what I did. I went to the world to get someone to want me around and for someone to see me. I hated the feeling of losing my God-mom, but it is what it was, and that was supposed to happen to me.

Chapter 3

LOOKING FOR LOVE

I got married and had my second daughter before I left the church, but it wasn't really a love thing. It was more of a getting married thing, because everyone put pressure on him because we were supposed to be saved. Jasmin is what I named her, and she brought joy to my heart. I thought that I could love now and at least half way take care of my daughters now (or so I thought), something I really did not know how to do with my first daughter, Vashon.

I cannot ever remember any time that I spent with Vashon and her dad together, not all three of us together. Therefore, with my second child, her father was there with us and we bonded over our child. I knew for a brief moment how it felt to have a real family. Nevertheless, we were young and that did not work out either. Now, I have two children and I was a ball of hurt and confusion. I wanted to know why no one I wanted to love ever loved me back! The anger that I felt at this time was massive! What was it about me that I didn't deserve to be loved? Why couldn't anyone I loved stay with me? Why did they have to go? Didn't they know I need them? Why, Why, Why? All I wanted was to be loved by someone, but I guess he was right again. I had just better be lucky to get anyone to love or be with me. So what is love then? Love is pain of course. Love is supposed to hurt. This is just the way it is supposed to be and that's' it, that's the way it goes! Therefore, I took my pain, or the love that I had known, and set out on a journey without my kids in mind.

How could I be a mother when I never really knew what it was to be one? I emulated what I was taught and I am sure my mother did the same.

Someone introduced me to crack; I don't even think I can remember who now. It was rolled up in weed, so I wasn't gonna turn into nobody's crack head, because it was in weed, and smoking it that way allowed me to stay awake longer and drink.

Drinking was what I did. Drinking was me. I was a drink and a drink was me. You didn't see Sharon without her drink! So not long after that, I was introduced to what we called 'primos'. I found out I was not a real fan of weed. No ma'am, I didn't want it, or was it that I wanted to do the crack only? I wanted to drink, and when I got drunk I wanted to smoke crack, because it allowed me to stay awake so that I could keep drinking without passing out. It was as if I found my non-stop, feel good party! Yay, I could drink all the time now. I wasn't about to give up alcohol. I knew I could always go to the store, drink, and feel better about anything that bothered me. People would leave me, but I didn't have to worry about them, because the alcohol would relieve me. I just had to go buy more. Look, alcohol was not going to leave me ever! It was not going to leave me in pain. Right? Funny thing about crack though, it doesn't want anything to come before it. They didn't tell me that I wouldn't be able to stop when I wanted to, or that I wouldn't be able not to want it either. I wanted it and now money was a problem. I ran the streets all the time. I always came back home though, but I had to get drunk and high. I could no longer do one without the other, they were a package deal and that was beginning to become costly. I would spend all my hard-earned money before the weekend was up and then I needed more. My memory from this period of my life is spotty at best, but what I do remember is I needed to stay stress-free!

I just wanted love, any love, someone to love me. And since I could not get it from a man, I would get it from a woman. I thought that I would try a woman. I mean surely it has to be better than being with a man, right? It seemed that women could understand each other better and women get along better than they do with men, so I tried it. I was so sick of being hurt by men and surely this was the answer for me to find real true love. I met someone and she made me feel great. I was happy for about a month! Literally, oh well, I figured I would stay with her, because at least she will not leave me for another, right?

Women wouldn't do women the way men treat women, would they? This relationship lasted about a year and I found out that some women are not too different from men, and that women cheat too. Of course, it didn't help that we both got high most of the time. Well, getting high is what attracted me to her anyway, two hurting individuals, and I needed some drugs and she had them, so we became lovers. I found out that her habit was much more intense than mine was and I slowly began to increase my drug use. It was horrible! All we did was 'eat and get high'. I got very tired of this lifestyle, but I was also stuck. I stayed in this relationship longer than I should have, and I ignored all unction that told me to get out as soon as I can. I just did not want to be alone. I would have given anything not to be alone! I stayed high just to stay in the relationship and I was very unhappy. We started arguing and fighting over drugs and this was enough. I have since learned that one should never pretend as if things are okay if "in fact, they are not." This will only lead to your demise! Get out! Now! I stayed for all the wrong reasons and ignoring my instincts only led me to more pain, pain that I would have to live with for the rest of my life. I wanted to be loved so bad that I ignored all that was wrong, and that cost me. It cost me my mind, as I got deeper into drugs. Drugs had me and I wanted to stay there. I did not want to come out and I didn't think I would ever recover from this relationship.

This was the angriest time of my life; I was fighting all the time and it didn't matter who I fought. I would fight men and women without any thought. All you had to do was cross me and it was over! I never picked a fight, but you had better not try to start one either. The rage I was feeling at this time of my life was crazy, I would go to the car wash, a place I hung out at and where I bought and sold drugs. This is where I did most of my arguing/fighting. It was nothing to get into an argument with someone, because I thought everyone was out to do me harm and try to get me, so I had to protect me. Well, my behavior was getting out of hand, so I had to chill on all the fighting I was doing in my life. I stopped fighting so much and I turned it inward. I thought that if I kept what I felt to myself, it would make things better. Well it only made me worse; I imploded on me. I turned the anger on myself and that was no good. I started to hate me and everything that I was. I was no good, nothing, and that is what I believed. "How could I be anything good?" is what I would tell myself. No one wanted to be with me; neither men nor women, so I had to be no good, right? I just stayed high in order to deal with the rage I had now turned on myself.

Chapter 4

STRESS RELIEF

Alcohol, Alcohol, Alcohol! Wow, I could drink and not have to worry about a thing! When I felt good, I was free of wanting anyone to love me. I could party and dance and people would look at me. I drank until my heart was content, but I was noticing something, I did not want to stop drinking. However, we all know that if you drink too much, you will become impaired, and I did not like that feeling. After a while, I was getting so drunk that I would black out while driving. I am most positive that I am alive today because of the grace of God! I should have died many times driving drunk. However, He spared me, and others that were on the road with me. Wow, I am grateful!

By this time, alcohol and drugs had become the most important thing in my life. I mean I lived them, breathed them. I just loved to drink! I could say what I really wanted to say. I could be whomever I chose to be for the day, hour, or whatever. I got what we used to call "liquid courage"! And it felt so good. Should I say, "Too good?"

I had the drug dealers on speed dial and they knew when I got paid, so they would front me drugs until payday. I was one of their best customers they would say, because I had a job! And in those days, that made me feel like I was better than most drug addicts were, because I mean dang, I got a job and most people know that crack heads can't hold a job right? Or so you thought! I had a job most of my drug addicted life, until I lost control. See, I thought I would just go on forever going to work hung over and feeling like crap all day, trying my best not to look like I have a hangover every day. But I knew they figured something was up. Therefore, I would get fired or quit from most jobs and that made me feel like I was messing up (really). So, I got this bright idea that I should work for a temporary agency. That way I would not have to feel bad when I couldn't go in, because I wanted to stay up and use drugs all night long. I would take job assignments when I wanted to and when I was too hung over, I wouldn't answer the phone. Problem fixed, right? No!

Eventually, that did not work anymore. My drug use began to get more and more out of control. I mean, I wanted to drink and I wanted to smoke and no one was going to tell me that I couldn't either! What I wanted I usually got, but what would I do to get it? Turns out a whole hell of a lot! I was introduced to a new way to make money ... I love it when you call him "PIMP DADDY!" (Or wait, did I?)

So I would go out to drink as I always would before I got high, because it made me feel like I was just like everybody else. Only when they went home, I went and got high. Therefore, while their party ended, mine was just getting started. I ran into this guy I had met at the car wash where me and my sister used to hang out at, or should I say at the "drug wash"… lol. Anyway, I knew he was a pimp and I didn't want any parts of that life. I mean really, why would you go and sell your body and give the money you earned on your back to a man, so he could look like he was important? That was just plain stupidity! We started talking and the more I drank, the more he was looking fine to me. We left there and I wanted to get high so bad, but I actually wanted to be with him more. Now this was different, the attention he gave me was all I needed. So we started to go out more and more, and he was a gentleman to me. He would take me around his other pimp friends and we would have a good time. I would see him when I was hanging out. He would be taking his girls and dropping them off to make money and it never really bothered me, because that was what he did and I was digging this dude now for real. A friend of mine would tell me, "You need to leave him alone," and I would tell him to mind his business cause I am grown! (That statement always seemed to get me into trouble; I didn't realize it then, but I see it so clearly now.)

Me? In love with a pimp? I mean, I was doing better then. I didn't smoke as much because I was with him most of the time. He wouldn't really let me out of his sight and those drug dealers, I knew, wouldn't let me buy from them when he was anywhere around. It was as if they all knew that J's girls were off limits to drug dealers. But I wasn't one of his girls was I? I never was a prostitute, for him. The attention that this man gave me made me feel like I could do anything; I could to breathe again. He loved me and he wanted me. He was always buying me things and he told me that if I want to be with him, I had to be clean. No more drugs for me! I could drink; that's all we would do every day, and every night we were in a bar somewhere getting drunk. One day he wanted me to go with him to pick up some money, and I did. When I saw how much money these girls were getting I was shocked, and I wanted some too!

He told me that I was the only girl he had with a regular job and that was cute, but I was being used by the white man. I was making peanuts and going to work hung over and that was not a good look. He told me that I would always be looking for another job, and that if I worked with him, I wouldn't have to work during the day. I could sleep in with him and we could be together more. I wasn't going for what he was saying, so he started disappearing. He wouldn't answer my calls; he would do things like drive right by me and wouldn't as much as honk. I mean I'd been with this man for about two months now and he would just drop me! Just like that! I was so hurt, so I went back to crack! When he heard I was smoking again, he came to me and told me that he could help me. I wanted to believe him so bad, because I thought I was doing so well with him. Therefore, we started dating again, but he became very demanding. I had to do this and I had to do that or else he would leave me again and I would go back to crack. "Is that what you want?" He would ask me. And he would tell me how he had changed my life and that I was looking better now, because I had gained a little weight. I was feeling a little better about myself now and it was because of his investment in me (wait a minute what investment?). Oh, but I didn't catch that statement though.

It's D-day now! Either 'you gonna do what I say or I am gone'! I didn't want to lose what I had, so I did it. I'm a 'hoe' now! The first day he dropped me off on Aurora I was scared. This was outside of my comfort zone, but I did it anyway. I made good money that night, but the next night I got popped! I tried to call him over and over again to come and get me, but he wouldn't answer me. I was pissed off! Now he told me what to do if this happened and that he would be there immediately to get me out. He said his girls don't stay in jail! Well, I was there for a day and a half!

I finally got back to the wash where we all hung out at and he was there laughing and smiling! I asked him why he didn't come get me. He smiled and said that I hadn't made enough money for him yet, and that he had invested a lot in me, and I got caught not him. Ride it out. He said it will be alright. He told me to get something to eat and be ready by nine. All in one breath! I couldn't really talk back, because that was a code of the pimp world. When your pimp was talking, especially to you around other pimps, you had better not say a word. So I turned and walked away for good, or so I thought!

I got the bright idea that if I was going to lay down for money it darn sure ain't going to be for no man! I would do it for myself and that is just what I did! So I started turning tricks on my own; I was making some money. However, not like out on Aurora, these tricks down on Rainier only wanted to pay you a little bit of money, so I had to turn more tricks to get money. After about a week of this and my so-called man being mad at me, it was too much for me to handle. So back to the crack it was and now, I could deal with how I felt when I did these awful things with these men. I was so high one night that I got into a trick's car, but I was too paranoid, so I had him take me to a park. We walked through the park into the bushes and that is where we did it! I mean this man could have killed me.

What was I doing to myself? He left me there and I walked back to the block to get even higher. A couple of weeks later, I got into a man's car and he had a baby asleep in the back seat! Really, oh hell no! I didn't even see the child at first, because I was so high, so I told him to let me out. He said, "Hoe, you are gonna do what I tell you to and you better be quiet." He had automatic locks and he locked the door and pulled out a knife. I did what he wanted me to do, but I was so scared while I was doing it, because I did not know if he was going to stab me in the back of my neck or what. When I was done, he told me to get out! I had a very long walk back to the avenue that night. I told one of the other girls what happened and identified what the car looked liked so we could pass it on to the other girls on the street so they would not get in the car with this maniac! She felt bad for me and gave me some crack so I wouldn't think about it anymore. We got high and went right back to turning tricks. We had a buddy system this time, and we would watch each other's backs (well, when we were around). See, now I had to stay drunk and high, because I couldn't handle what I was doing and how it made me feel inside. I could not even look at myself in the mirror anymore, literally.

I decided to go have some drinks one night and there he was, my boyfriend, or was he my pimp? He was kind of mad at me. I could tell because the first thing he said to me was "I hear you are a renegade?" "Huh, what? What does that mean?" I asked. He said, "It's a hoe out here in these streets with no protection and getting money from these tricks without guidance." I smiled and said, "Yeah, I guess if that's what you call it. I mean you left me in jail." He didn't like that I said that, especially with his pimp friends at the table. Nevertheless, he asked me to sit down, so I did. He gave me permission to talk and have a good time with him and his boys, so I did that too. He was ordering double shots of Couvassie and I was drunk up! I had to go to the bathroom, but I hadn't finished my drink and a rule of the streets is 'never leave your drink unattended'! But I knew him, right? We were lovers before; he was cool, so I left him to watch over my drink. I came back and he asked me if I want to get a room and I said okay. I was so drunk. He told me to finish my drink and we would leave. I felt like we might have a chance again; I really did not want to smoke crack anymore, but I had to do something to contain my feelings, because they were just too strong for me to handle.

We pulled up to the motel (let's keep it real) and the next thing I remember was him telling me to get up. What...what just happened? All I felt was pain inside and it hurt to walk. I looked at him and he smiled and said, "Did you think I wouldn't get my money from you?" "So what did you allow to happen to me?" I asked. He told me "shut up and let's go". I will never forget that day ever! So what happened to me? Did he trick me out all night and me not even know about it? Did he let strange men in this room and I never knew; I mean what happened to me last night? Devastated, betrayed, lost, hurt, abandoned, pissed, mad, and angry!!! All these I felt inside. So let's go get high!

FLASHY, MONEY-MAKING MAN!
(Poem)

You know you see him all out in those streets. You know him, can't miss him, cause you hear his beats. The sound of his music is so good to your ears.

He gets out of his ride and smiles real big and wide, as if to say everything is good in my hood today. But what you didn't hear or know is that the tapping of his toe was a sign to tell you that he is nervous for sure!

Oh you thought he was smiling at you…Oh you think it's all good? Tap, Tap, Tap goes his toe. So you ask him can I go? He smiles real wide and says yes, come let's ride.

Now you're rolling to his hood not realizing that greedy smile comes for your demise. But you don't see it; all you hear is the music in your ears. Did he tell you that at night the music goes off!? Did he tell you that his smile goes down when the sun begins to set? He puts on his game face, no time to rest.

Flashy Money Making Man, are you too true to be good? Do you get what you see or do you do what he tells you? Shssh be quiet now, night time is coming, the smile is gone the music is a humming...now you're riding through his hood at a real great cost. Yeah, It's going to cost you, it'll cost your mind, your will, and your emotions.

Now it's up to you if you're still thinking about going. So you roll out with him anyway, is what you decide to do, you roll with him cause he's so fine and he wants you! What you don't know and what you do not seem to understand is that this man is dangerous and so are his plans.

The devil in disguise if you want to call him that, either way it goes he wants you on your back! Oh yea he wants you, yes he does indeed. He wants what you can do for him, but that you couldn't see.

So this ride with this man has cost you a lot. Oh you want to be that ride or die chick? Well you just might get what you want. So what will you do the next time you hear the music, the next time you see that smile and that grin? The next time that Flashy Money Making Man shows up on your street again?

Well may I make a suggestion based on my experience? Go back inside and ignore the smile; don't even think about getting into his ride! The things he wants to give serve you no purpose; it's only for his greed and social posture. So please take heed to what you have read and maybe even seen; this type of man only comes with the devil's plans indeed.

Chapter 5

REHAB…MOTHER…MARRIAGE

I was out of control and I could not hide the fact that I bought crack! I needed it and by now, I didn't care who knew. Well, I did care because I was trying to hide it, but it was not working. I knew I needed help, because I would darn near do just about anything to get high. I did everything you could possibly think of. I was a prostitute for a little bit of money, I sold drugs, and I rolled game on whoever would buy it. Some things I will leave to the imagination, but let's just say the things I did, I can never take back and my mind always remembers.

I went to rehab like three times and I tried to kill myself. I almost overdosed and I still went back to using. I guess going back and forth to rehab doesn't really instill in people that you are going to make it. I had no chance with this woman before I started using, so why on earth did I think I had a chance now? But I did for some reason, and it was false hope. I left my children with my mom while I was in and out of rehab and on and off drugs. One thing I knew was that she would make sure they ate and that they were clothed. But the thing that I was unsure of was if she would turn them against me or not show them love. She was so mad at me that she would tell me the kids weren't home when they were, and I get that part, because she had to deal with the crying when I didn't come home. I really didn't care what my mom had to go through, because I felt like she wanted me to use. I was her excuse to get sympathy, because mom had to have attention. I would try to get her to see that all I wanted was her love.

From the time I was a child I just wanted my mom, but she would not give me her. She fed me, clothed me, housed me, and brought me to church, but I wanted more than that. I needed her love. All the pain and the emptiness I felt was too much for me. I needed her to help me figure this out, but she ignored me. It seemed as if there was nothing I could do to make this woman love me, so I said, "Forget it!" I had to take responsibility for getting strung out, but I felt that she pushed me to it. I had this idea that I wouldn't smoke any more, but I needed my drink to be happy, because now everyone knew I was a crack head and my mom was definitely going to make sure that everyone knew it too. Now, she really hated me. There were times when I wouldn't even be doing anything (this is when I got out of treatment) and she would pick fights with me just to see if I would leave and go get high. It felt as if she was pushing me out once again! Well I was the crack head remember. Therefore, I deserved to be treated any kind of way since I was the bottom of the barrel. If you smoked crack, you were the worst drug addict ever! All I remember is feeling alone and mad at the world! So my sobriety didn't last. Now I was determined to stay high, because church doesn't work, the streets don't work, and I don't work. So forget it all! Now I am a full-fledged addict. I had to survive and I needed to stay High! Yep, bottom of the barrel is where I resided.

Then I met another man who I thought loved me. He took good care of me and gave me everything my heart desired. I didn't have to want for anything. He took care of me and my kids. I mean, what more could a woman of my background want?

I took him to my God mom's house and she told me that everything that shines is not gold and my reply was, "I got this mom," and I left in that black Cadillac with that man to embark upon a journey that would surely change my life.

(I can remember walking away from the house that she was at when she told me that).

He helped me to stay sober for a while. I stayed clean and sober, I was proud of myself, and I thought my mom would be too. But now I was living in sin and that was a problem too. She was never really happy with me then either. Deep down inside I was angry with my mom, but at the same time, all I wanted was her love and approval.

So we got married! We had a son...the son I always wanted. He knew how bad I wanted a boy, and he knew I would do anything for him as well. It was nice to have a husband who "loved me for me" (because by the way, he was one of my tricks) so I didn't have to hide anything from him at all. He knew everything there was to know about me. He helped me to try to forgive the feelings I had towards my mom, but the feelings I had would not go away easily.

See, it's hard to forgive if you are still being hurt repeatedly. He would watch as she ignored every positive thing I did. I still wanted my mom's love, but it was proving harder to get it. Thus, I tried to forget about her, once again. I was so dependent on this man. He used to smoke too, so he knew what he is doing, and I followed his lead. He showed me that I could sell crack and not have to smoke it, and to me if you used to smoke crack and now you sold it you were the strongest person in the world. I thought I was so strong to beat the odds, because everyone told me that people who smoke always go back and even in treatment. They told us that the success rate for crack smokers was slim to none. What a concept to instill in the minds of those who walk away from treatment!

My husband was my rock. He sold crack on the side, and he and I worked, and we seemed to be working out for a while, until I got a real job making real money. I was hired as a truck driver for the post office and I made good money. I loved my job, but he didn't like it because he was no longer my only source of confidence, and I could buy things for myself. Now I felt good about myself and I thought that would make him happy, but it didn't; he actually started to hate me. Huh? What? I was really confused now.

So what happens when your husband starts to question everything you do and while you are doing them, it makes you leery of him? He started to change and he wasn't the man I could trust anymore. Instead, he became this obsessive, crazy man and it happened all of a sudden too, or did I just ignore the little signs along the way? I remember waking up and getting ready to go to work and he was sitting up staring at me, and it scared me. I said, "What are you doing?" I tried to move him out of my way so I could get up, but he pushed me into the closet and told me that I wasn't going anywhere. I was like, "What? What is wrong with you?" He looked crazy in his eyes and I knew then I was in trouble and I hated the feeling of being trapped. I could not stand it! Therefore, I begged him to let me out of the closet and that I would do anything he asked. I started to go to the bathroom to get dressed for work, but he told me he already called them and told them that I wasn't coming in. Now I knew he was crazy. I tried everything I could to reassure him...that I was in love with him, that I didn't want any other man at my job or anything, and that I was happy with my family, but he wasn't convinced. He wanted the weak, strung-out girl that he met who was dependent on his every move, and that girl was gone.

He started to follow me everywhere I went and the constant stalking was too much for me to handle, so I went back to what made me happy... drinking. My cousin and I could drink up a storm and I suddenly remembered why I used to drink...so I could be happy. Once again, I could deal with his madness for as long as I was drunk, so I stayed that way all the time. But I was a truck driver and I needed to be able to stay awake. I was growing very afraid of him. He was becoming very unpredictable now. He would show up at the bar in his pajamas and yell across the room, "SHARON, SHARON, TIME TO COME HOME!" He would embarrass me to death! Now I was starting to hate him, but I knew he was for real crazy and I didn't know what to do, so I stayed drunk and tried to ignore him. He mentally tormented me and I was scared to do anything. Now I wanted out! I didn't want to smoke crack anymore, but drinking wasn't enough to bear what I was going through, so I started to pop pills this time. I mean I almost died!

One night while trying to escape his madness, I drank nine mini bottles of tequila and took two blue 'number 10' valiums. I just did not want to think anymore. I survived this night only by the grace of God. In my effort to forget, I would stay out late until he had to go to work, then I would go home to get some rest (since he wouldn't let me sleep if I was there with him.) I detested that life and couldn't live like that anymore. I believe he sensed it. He didn't come home one night and I was kind of scared but I was like, "Okay, maybe he found someone else and he will not be thinking about me so much", and I was fine with it. Except that when he came home, he looked like a mad man! He had smoked crack! OMG! Now it was really time to go. I could handle him crazy, but not 'crack crazy'. Oh no ma'am! I know the constant fighting had to be unbearable for my children. I was simply trying to keep us together as a family, but enough was enough. My daughter could not handle it anymore, because I worked nights and slept days. The nights I was off, I was out getting drunk and she was the live-in baby sitter. I was so wrong for placing that kind of responsibility on her. For that, I apologize. In the midst of all these craziness, I did not know that my daughter wanted to run away, and that my mother, of all people, was going to be the one to help orchestrate the runaway. Huh? Not once did she even think of calling me to tell me that my daughter was thinking about running away. For real! She could have called me and told me that my daughter needs me and that she wants to leave. What my mother did tell my daughter was that when I go to sleep, she, my daughter, should flick the lights on and off, and she, my mother, will pull up in the alley and she was to jump the fence and run to her. As if she was being held hostage! Why didn't she call my daughter's dad and tell him what she was feeling? Little did I know that my mom had a serious problem with attention, and that she would soon prove to do WHATEVER she could to get that?

So now my daughter was gone in the middle of the night and I was frantic. I am calling the police and everybody else, yet my mom does not tell me until the next day that my daughter was with her the entire time. What is that? I thought somebody kidnapped her, hell we all did! She had her all the time? What! What!!! I was confused. That hurt me to my core! Now my husband is a psychopathic crack head, my daughter is gone, my mother lied to me, and I am scared out of my brains! Knowing that I had to leave him for real because of how badly it has affected my daughter truly devastated me. I was too drunk and pilled out to even think about how all this was affecting my children. I only thought about my happiness, and nothing else seemed to matter!

He never touched my children, by the way. I would not allow him to touch my girls ever! He would have surely died if he did, and I think he knew that. I was just absolutely fed up with his possessiveness, accusations, and his controlling nature.

I remember snapping one day and taking all of his finest suits and gator shoes, putting them on the grill and setting them on fire! Oh, I felt so good! It was a "waiting to exhale" moment! I was tired of being scared of him and I was going to show him. I told him to come home quickly and eat something special I prepared for him. He looked scared when he walked in the door, I mean for real! I sat him at the table and told him to eat what I specially made for him. He looked around and wondered why we were not eating. I told him we were fine and that I just wanted to watch him eat. Well, he never touched his food, but I won a very important battle that week, because now he thought I was crazy too. If you can bring it, I can bring it too. Yeah, try me; I am crazy too boo! Then he took his crazy to the next level. He started to use my son as a bargaining tool. He kidnapped him and told me he could take him away at any given time. He called me when he took him and let me hear him cry. I told him anything I could to get my son back to me. I was afraid of losing my children again! The last thing I wanted was to ask my mom for help. I mean she just helped my daughter run away, but I didn't have any other options. I had to get my other two kids out of this situation. She was the only option I could think of and I hated her! I really did not want her to get my kids.

He backed off for a while, not knowing that I was still planning my escape. One night, I took my kids and we went to my cousin's house where we thought we would be safe, but I woke up to this man standing over me, asking why I was not home. I looked around and called out to my cousin. She came and said, "How did you get in here?" I mean, my cousin's place is on the third floor. She looked at the front door, it was locked, and we made sure it was locked. We hid my car so he wouldn't think we were there. We took every precaution, except we didn't think to lock the balcony door. I mean, really, we are on the third floor! THIS MAN CLIMBED THE BUILDING TO GET INTO HER APARTMENT TO SEE IF WE MIGHT BE THERE? WOW!!! I knew I was in trouble, but I didn't know what to do. He found us! Even if I continued to try to leave several times, this man would continue to find us. I was so frustrated. I was about to lose my job and could no longer take everything that was going on. I was dragging my kids around from house to house trying to hide from this man. Yes, I did have restraining orders, yes, I did call the police, and yes, he always got out on some sort of mix up or technicality. I could not handle the running away anymore. It didn't matter anyway, since he would just find me.

He convinced me that he would change, that we would go to church, and that he would make it work. I bought into it because in the process of all this, I had lost my job. Well, that change lasted a short time and then I could not even talk on my phone anymore. I had to go to the room when he told me to. I had to do what he said at all times. This time I was so done! I think he knew it, though he couldn't take the chance of me running away again, because this time, he might not find me.

I had no one else that I knew who would take care of my kids but my mom. She had a daycare and the kids would be well taken care of. I DID NOT WANT TO ASK HER TO HELP ME, BUT I NEEDED TO GET MY KIDS OUT OF THIS MADNESS. WE WERE ALWAYS RUNNING FROM HIM AND I WAS TIRED! So, I did and she came and got them. I kissed them and cried. All I wanted to do was get them to a safe place and I knew he would not go there. He and my mom did not really ever like each other. I gave up my kids up to a woman I could not trust, but knowing that they would be safe there, I did.

The next day, I was sitting in an empty apartment that was in shambles. He had been gone and I asked a dealer who I knew to help me move 'ASAP,' and he did. I went back the next day to get some other things. As I was in the back room, I heard the front door open. My heart dropped! "He is here. How do I get out?" I thought to myself. I heard voices and he was with another man and a girl. They were all happy and he had a briefcase in his hand. He was smiling, so I thought I would be safe. He told me he wanted me to come with him, but I told him that I was leaving. He then said that I wasn't going anywhere but with him. He grabbed me by the arm and shoved me in the car. I was scared, but I didn't know what to do. We went to a motel and before we got out of the car, he pulled a knife out and said, "You better not tell anyone." He said, "We are going to walk in here and get a room and you better say nothing." He held my arm so close and I looked at the girl, but she just turned her head. We got into the room and we started to drink. He knew that I loved vodka and he had plenty. We got drunk, and as I was getting sleepy, he told me that he had something for me. I was like, "What!" I knew what it was, and I had done really good about not going back to crack. I may have started drinking again and popping pills, but at least I wasn't smoking. He told me that I was going to smoke or else! The things that happened to me in that room I will leave un-spoken at this time.

The next day I begged him to get me something to eat. At first, he said "No!" But I told him I was starving and that I wouldn't try to run away. He finally agreed and we walked next door. He still had this knife under my arm and told me not to try anything. We got into the waiting room of the restaurant and I looked around. I saw a group of young people that seemed very happy, and they were because they were talking about Jesus! I remember looking into this young girl's eyes, and for some reason we connected instantly! She sensed that something was very wrong. She started to walk up towards us and before I knew it she yelled, "Satan, I rebuke you in the name of Jesus!" I fell to the ground and he ran out of the restaurant. They called the police and ambulance and they also called my mother. They had three different police departments dispatched to look for him, because they knew whom they were dealing with. I had called the police several times before on this man and they never caught him, and they didn't catch him that time either! I was in the back of the ambulance talking to the police (This is very hard for me). The back door opens up and my mom is standing there with a look of disgust. What the hell? She is mad at me for this man kidnapping me? Hurt was not what I felt at that time. Instead, I felt something that hurt couldn't touch. It was beyond that and it does not have a name. She opened her mouth and the words I will never forget...not ever. The police officer looked at her with disgust and told her that was a horrible thing to say.

After that, I checked out mentally for a long time. I used drugs at an alarming rate. I drank every second I could, but I missed my kids so much. But I was so hurt. After sleeping in my car and just trying to survive, I realized that I wanted my kids so bad. I got myself cleaned up again and off drugs and I called my mom. I told her that I wanted my kids back, that I had a job, and that I was working on getting an apartment again. She kind of laughed and said, "Okay."

The day I went to go and pick up my kids she had gotten a restraining order and told the courts that I had disappeared, and she did not know where I was. AGAIN ... REALLY ... AGAIN? I think I was so angry this time that I was determined not to let her win. I jumped through so many hoops. I had to prove that I had not abandoned my kids, but that I asked my mom to take them because we were living in chaos and abuse. I had to get police reports to show the reason why I took my kids to my mom, so I could get them out of this situation and keep them safe. I had to get phone records to prove that I was in constant contact with her. I only stayed away, because I didn't want this man to take my son from me. I had to do a UA Drug Test to prove that I was not using, and I proved it. We went to court and to my surprise; no one was in favor of what she had done. This was a surprise, because my mom always made me feel like I was nothing; and that all I would ever be was a crack head! Well, no mother, not today!

The judge reprimanded my mother in a way that I have never heard before. Let's see if I can remember his words correctly. He told her "in all of his years as a judge, he never saw a mother fight so hard to keep a daughter away from her children." He recognized that I had had some issues in the past, but she should have been the main one cheering me on and it was unbelievable what she had done.

That day I felt so much relief. Finally, someone saw my mother for who she really was to me. I fought for my kids and I got them back.

MOTHER
(Poem)

You keep trying me don't you? You keep swinging at me
don't you? Why is it so important for you to make me feel
pain? You birthed me didn't you? So what is it about me that
makes you want to hurt me? What have I done since I was
born to make you hate me?

Wow! I have never seen until now the realization of the
pain you were creating. It makes me wonder how the one who
birthed you treated you this way. Wow!

See, your contention doesn't come from nowhere. It had to
been created in some form of despair. The evilness...the
wicked eyes...the ugliness from which you derive, nothing

moves you but pain. You see, it's the craziness and chaos that soothes you. What a way to live! What a way to grow...deceit and manipulation. That is not love. You spread it around like it is though, never realizing that pain is all you know. I am a grown woman now. I am indeed, no more having to feel like I need your approval, no more need for your disapproval.

See I am my Father's child and I have dominion over all that's negative...over all that you have done. It's me and my Father now and we are on the run--to correct the lies and indignation you have caused ...to cancel the so called debt you say I owe. See, my Father and I don't agree with your calculations. In fact, your books are rigged and we have come to replace them.

Chapter 6

BROKEN & LEAVING

I never really got back to me after that or what was me? I think what my mother did truly devastated me beyond what my mind could handle. I continued to drink and eventually, I wound up back smoking and selling crack again. But I kept my two youngest kids with me. However, my oldest never really came back after she ran away. Our relationship was never the same. My estranged husband finally went to prison for a year, but he got out and no one from our fine adult detention services told me before he got out. So, he found us and haunted us wherever we went. I could not get him out of my mind. I drank all day and smoked all night, because I was so afraid to go to sleep at night for fear that this fool would always find us. I mean, we moved probably four times in one year and I was sick of it! I wanted peace and I needed some real help. I wanted love and peace, and most of all I wanted me. I decided to move out of the state.

I could feel that my drug use was starting to try to take over again and I did not want that. I was able to hold down a job, sell crack, smoke crack, and drink. I could feel that the crack wanted me back on those streets and I had already done that and I was not going back. So I made up my mind it was time to leave and that is just what we did. My uncle and my cousin played a huge role in supporting me when I was at my lowest low! And I mean I had some kind of lows…whew weee! My lows where low, but these two individuals never judged me! They always told me it would be okay. My cousin, I will always love her to pieces. She was the air that I needed to breathe; she understood me some-how. She loved me, just me. My uncle took us to the train station and off we went.

Moving for Mistaken Love

I thought I would finally get it together here. Well I thought. I thought I would try to give my mom a chance to love me again. I was sure my sister was going to help and love me. I would be free from my past and this would be a new start. Well here we go; we are going to try it again. I was going to fight for my mom's love one more time. I was really scared about trying to love her again or even trying to let her back into my world; she is my mom and I wanted her to be a part of my life. It seems like I have spent most of my life fighting for my mothers' love and never being able to get it. I was going to try again, because deep inside, I believed that I could have the family that I had always dreamed of.

I would constantly think of my oldest daughter, but I knew she hated me. Our relationship was basically nothing, but deep in my heart, I wanted her and all my children to love me and respect me again. How in the world would I make this happen? I prayed all the time, "God please give me my family back, please." It just seemed too impossible, but I would continue to try. You know the house with the white picket fence? I wanted so much to believe that I could have a normal life, and that I could be with a good man who could love me for just me. Not for what I could do for him sexually. I wanted a mother who would take me out to lunch and we could hold hands and walk in the park or just sit and talk. I mean is that too much to ask for? It seems that up to this point, each time I try to trust someone with my heart, they fail me or I fail myself for allowing myself to give my heart away. Maybe I should just stay to myself, by myself, and not want love any more.

The most frustrating thing in the world is to want love, and not be able to get it. But I guess, maybe, I wasn't looking in the right places. I tried to get my mom to accept me again. I got a good job and I was going to church again, and this was the only time in my life when I felt that things would work out. Time had passed and we should have been able to work through our issues from the past. I tried to do that, but she still didn't seem to like me. I could never get her to just love me. I always felt like I was being judged on every side. Whatever I did was never enough, because if it were, my mom would love me. So I had to be doing something wrong again, right?

For a time, I felt as though I was in a time warp and that everything I had felt before regarding my mom had certainly resurfaced, and I lost it! I needed a drink to be complete and that's what I got. So my relationship with my mom did not get any better. I was disappointed to say the least, once again. Back to drugs and back to alcohol, but not back to the streets. I held down a job and got my own place while partying all the time, and I was able to keep a roof over our heads. The pain that I was feeling was extreme; I did not want to feel anything but happy.

If I was sober, it meant that I would have to face the rejection from my mother and the wanting to call her and say, "Hey I need you." I was not willing to do that again so I drank, and I drank at all costs.

If my mom wasn't going to love me, I would find someone who will! That's when I met him, through a friend of mine, and he became my dealer. In SC, I really couldn't find anyone that sold crack; it seemed as if everyone I knew snorted cocaine. I really didn't like snorting too much; it made me higher longer than I wanted to be. See, I liked to be in control when I got high and when I came down. Control freak? Naw, I just wanted to be in control of how I felt and what I felt. I did not think that was too much to expect from myself. Little did I know he sold crack! When I did get the cocaine, I would hold some until I was alone at home and try to cook it up, but it never really tasted or came out like I wanted it to. So, he sold crack too. Jackpot! But I won't overdo it; only on the weekends, I told myself. He was kind of surprised when I asked him if he did sell the hard stuff. I told him it was for my neighbor and at the time, that was partly the truth. He looked at me a little strange, but he gave it to me anyway. After a while, I stopped asking for the cocaine and only started buying crack, and then he knew. But I didn't really care, because I was still working and my bills were paid.

One night he asked me to come to his house and I said I would, but only if he cleared out his place, because I did not like to party in front of people. See my motto was, "If you didn't see me do it, then you can't say that I am doing it!" Come to find out, this was his motto as well. That was my story and I stuck to it. So I went, and boy oh boy, did we have a night to remember. Well anyway, after that night, we started to see each other here and there. He would take me out to eat and he would spend time with me and my kids. Well, I really thought he liked me. He wanted to know why I never spent time with my family. So I began to tell him what I have previously told you. He was so angry with them. To me, it was as if he was superman the way he took up for me against my mother. My children and I were treated differently. We weren't invited to some family events on the holidays, excuses were made, etc. I would get so mad that my mom could spend time with church folks, but would not ask us.

No, I am not perfect, but does that exclude me from being loved? Do my actions of drug use exclude me from family events, because of their shame of who I was? But they could call me when they wanted me for something and I was acceptable then. Of course, there were some events that I was allowed at, but really, who wants to be wanted at someone else's expense? I was made to believe that if I was not who they wanted me to be, then I was undeserving of their time and affection. I was only a crack head! So having him in my life was what I needed and I was unwilling to give that up. He would ask me every holiday to come with him and his family or we would plan something on our own. At the time, his family consisted of a live-in friend who was an ex-girlfriend that he was trying to get rid of, but for some obvious reason, he could not. She really didn't want him. She just wanted his dope and money, and if he put her out, he would be sold out. He was unwilling to take that chance, because he made a lot of money. There is no way that I am going to live with a man and allow his so-called real girlfriend to come over when she wanted, (or would I?) I didn't really care about her at the time either, because I wanted to get high and I didn't get high around him. So I was fine, as long as I could have him when I wanted him. He could not believe what I had been through, until he saw it with his own eyes.

Did my mom have reason to still hate me? I don't know. You decide. Was I a drug user? Yes, I was. Was I wrong for drinking the way I did? Yes, I was. Did that disqualify me from love? Oh no, ma'am! So by this time, all I wanted was love, and this man was showing me what I thought was love at the time. The problem was that he had the live in ex-girlfriend and the other girls. And those girls wanted him and they would do whatever they could to get him. Because you know, he was the man. He was pretty prosperous at his drug dealings and everybody knew him, so I felt real special being his main girl. Yep, I said it, "Main girl," which apparently meant that I had him most of the time, and the other times they got him. So I convinced myself that this would be okay, because he started to want me to stop using, but I didn't want to, because that is how I kept the pain at a distance. I just couldn't give that up. I had to come up with something to keep using, so I think we had come to an unspoken agreement that he could have his little flings with these girls, if I could smoke. Hence, that's how we lived, and he didn't say anything about me using and I couldn't say anything about those girls! When I was with him, he kept the pain at a distance, but then when he had to go do what he had to do, I had to have something to keep the pain away.

This vicious cycle kept me in bondage and hell for a very long time, one that I was willing to live in order to keep feeling as though everything was alright. That worked for a while, until I noticed that I wanted him more than the drugs. However, since I had already agreed to this rule, I had a hard time convincing this man that I wanted him and not what he could give me. That, I guess, was when he started testing me. He stopped giving me drugs and I couldn't even buy them. What? "Umm okay, so you want me to stop, how about you?" I asked him. That did not go over so well, because he wanted me to prove to him that I was going to stop using, without any conditions. All the girls he was dealing with were using and they were all using him for what he had. In return, he got what he wanted. So am I willing to give up my painkiller to get a new painkiller? This would require me to be without either painkillers from time to time. Wow! I guess I do love this man. I tried to stop using several times, but he was always out on a run with someone, so when he did that, I would sneak and go get high. I would get if from another dealer who really wanted me. I thought this was cute that I could have both worlds. When my dude was out messing around, I would just call the other one, right? Well, what one has, the other one wants to brag about.

So eventually, he found out that I was dealing with this dude and he did not like that at all. It was as if I had done the unthinkable, but he was still messing with those girls, so who cared right? Well he did, and I had to stop if I wanted to keep him, and so I did. I guess I loved him more than getting high and I wanted him more than I wanted to get high. He had become my new drug, my painkiller, and I wanted him more than anything in this world! I didn't care what this man did, and he did a lot. All I wanted was him, because I could stay clean if he was with me, except that he had a painkiller too. And it was alcohol!

I decided to drink with him. The only problem with that was when I got drunk, I craved drugs. So, we had devised a plan that I would have to eat before I got too loaded, because if I ate, then I would get sleepy and go to bed. He really wanted me to stop using, so I tried and tried, but it was not working. I just hid it from him. I mean how was he going to ask me to stop? I had a job, and I only got high at night and he was a drug dealer. Really! So I told him that if he stopped, I would stop. He eventually did.

Drug dealers were getting popped left and right around our hood and it was time for him to stop. By then, I hardly used drugs, but it was still there with me just in case I would need a painkiller. I wanted his love more than I wanted the drugs anyway. The drugs only numbed me from what I did not have, and now that he loved me, I did not need drugs as much. But he still had some stragglers that where hidden as well, therefore, I was going to stop for real now and maybe he would let those stragglers go. That is when I traded drugs and alcohol for what I thought was love, only to find out that the pain he would cause me would only drive me back to my first painkiller.

He could never really give up his vices either. He hid them and he lied to me. He was cheating on me repeatedly. I thought this man was mine, all mine, all the while ignoring every sign. I was hooked on him though and I wasn't going to let him go, so I settled for less. I settled for a mess! I became entangled in the pain of wanting what I could not have and that pain was too much to bear. My painkiller had now become the giver of pain. He worked nights as he had always done, so I didn't really see this one coming. He had moved in with his mother, because she had surgery and needed him. So, that was okay. He was working and taking care of his mother. What I didn't know was that he wasn't really staying with his mother, but was staying with another! When I found out, I was so devastated to say the least. But why? This was his "M.O.," but to have a whole other family that he was taking care of? This was crazy to me.

One thing that I did know about this man was that he was a sucker for a damsel in distress! Whenever one would call who needed a ride or didn't have a place to go, he would go out of his way to help them. Now I would not let myself believe that there was any other reason for him helping these girls, because if I did, then the pain would come back. This time the one he helped needed way more care than I had ever seen him give. The problem with this is that every time he would help one of these individuals, he would wind up getting screwed. He got a trailer for them to live in and moved most of his belongings in there, I mean they were living as a family and I didn't even know! So, I came up with this plan to try to stay sane. Here it goes. I spent time with him and pretended that I was the only one and when he left, I would go get drunk. When the drinking wasn't working to keep the pain at bay, I smoked crack to make it all go away. I would wake the next day feeling bad about the crack, I would call him up, and he would come back. Therefore, I got to feel a false sense of love for a short period of time, and when his phone rang for him to go to her; I would go get a dime. I lived this pattern for a very long time. I loved this man and I was not willing to let him go! I mean he was there for me when my mom was not. He made sure we didn't spend a holiday alone and hey, I was still using, so you gotta give something if you want something, right?

One thing I knew was that I needed to have two painkillers at all times, because you couldn't ever trust any one individual ever in life. Through all this turbulence of my life, the only thing I wanted was to keep the pain at bay. This had become my life's journey: trying to figure out how to keep the pain away. I did nothing else in life but this.

The phone rang one day and I had to go back to where it all started, Seattle! I did not want to go there, because I was afraid of being stalked again. What if he found us? But my daughter needed me and I had to go. I had no choice, so I told him I had to go, and I think that did something to us. We began to get closer! The girl and the trailer situation had blown up in his face, as I told him it would. And yes, I have to say I was pleased that it did. He started to show me that he wanted just me and I was happy about that, but I still had to leave. Really? Now, when I just got him to myself? Would he go or would I lose him again? Well, he said he would go, but he would have to return to check on his mom, and I said okay. My hopes for a good life were starting to appear. I may just finally get my family that I have always wanted.

The transition to Seattle was not going to be an easy one. We would have to move in with my daughter until I find a job. I was afraid of this because my daughter and I had not had a good relationship due to my drug and alcohol use. The last time she had really been in my care was when she was a teenager and that did not end so well. She never came back to me after she ran away that day. We were broken as a mother and daughter unit and I had no idea on how I could fix it either. I was still broken and hurting and I had mommy issues. She had mommy issues too, and we were going to be under one household, colliding, as we both carried the same issues. There would be no outside support, no counseling, and we would make it work. How can that be? I was frustrated, scared, and unsure of what God was doing and what the next chapter of my life would be. However, one thing I did know was that I was going to Seattle.

I always prayed to God whether I was high or not. For some reason, I believed that he heard me. That was pretty evident, because at every painful turn, He was there for me. I was always taken care of, and so were my children. I will always be grateful for that. I remember when individuals would call me on my phone when I didn't know how I was going to pay for my rent and they would tell me to come get money so I could pay my bills. One time, I was at a club and a guy that I knew looked me in my eye and told me I didn't belong in this kind of lifestyle and handed me the amount of my past due rent. I was constantly being provided for and I was not doing what I was supposed to be doing. I felt and still do feel that God was looking out for me and I had to find a way to say thank you to Him. I know this may sound strange. With all the things that happened to me, I should be mad at Him, right? Believe me I was. In my worst drug addict days, I hated God! I told Him I hated Him and I asked him over and over again why He was not allowing anyone to love me. I spent most of those years asking and begging Him to help me stop using and pleading with Him to take the pain away. Now, I believe that I went through what I went through to help someone else.

What I had coming for me in Seattle was another thing. I still loved God, but I knew that I was not doing what was right, so I did not feel adequate and deserving of His love either. I was taught what love was as a child and from what I have learned, love has stipulations, doesn't it? Yes it did, in my mind. The one thing that I knew I was deserving of was food and shelter. My mom had made sure that we had food and a roof. So maybe I thought that God was providing for me through these different individuals, because that is what He was supposed to do. So I wasn't really looking for Him to do more than that.

Chapter 7

FACING FEAR & ADDICTION

So I moved back to Seattle where it all started. Man was I scared! I did not know if my son's father had totally given up on me. That was one of the biggest reasons why I moved out in the first place, other than trying to get clean.

I got on that plane anyway, knowing full well that I may live in fear again...or maybe not! How about I stop running from what he has done to me and face reality? So I did! And I faced him and was not afraid.

I came back to Seattle still smoking and drinking, but God was still pulling at my heart. The everyday vicious cycle of using, drinking, and popping pills had begun to take its toll on my life. I couldn't drink like I wanted to and the drugs weren't getting me to the place that I wanted to get anymore. I was just plain miserable. My South Carolina man came and stayed, left, came and stayed again, and then left. I really thought that we had a chance. I mean I knew he had to help take care of his mom, or that was what I kept telling myself. Each time he left to go home, I would have the most horrible feeling in my gut...one that I would always brush away. Then the phone games started.

He wouldn't answer all night until the next day! We already had serious trust issues and this was not helping, but for some reason, I allowed myself to believe that I could hold on until he came back. And I did, and when he came back, he was good, but when he left, he was bad. The pain and agony of wanting someone, anyone to love you can make you feel as if you are an addict. It is the wanting of something so bad that you are willing to do anything to keep that feeling of love...the feeling that makes you smile and makes you think that everything is going to be alright.

People will spend hours just trying to make themselves feel wanted, approved, and cared for. We spend thousands of dollars making ourselves feel good. We can even make ourselves believe just about anything we want. So why cannot we use this powerful suggestion of our mind to make ourselves believe that we are beautiful ... that we are approved, needed, and relevant? Why do we need some outside force to validate who we are and who we are to be?

We will stay in a horrible relationship and allow someone to lie to us and abuse us, because our fear of being without love and acceptance is so strong that we will do anything to keep those feelings. Our emotions are more powerful than we realize, so how do we control them? Is it just an issue of mind over matter? Is it just making ourselves believe that we can succeed? But what happens when that overwhelming feeling of loneliness comes to stalk us? We yield to the urge of not wanting those feelings, and then we produce whatever we need to make those unwanted feelings go away.

I believe what I have just described is addiction, and society deems addictions as drugs and alcohol. However, I believe that we must look at another addiction that is not talked about as much, and that is emotional addiction. I view emotional addiction as the "feel good" addiction, very much the same as any other addiction. Too bad society does not talk about emotionally addicted people that much. Women will stay in an abusive relationship just so they do not have to feel the feelings of abandonment and rejection–feelings or state of beings that promote hell on earth for certain individuals. We will stalk someone, not knowing that this will turn them away, because the need to feel wanted is so great. Individuals do not care what is at stake. The temporary need to feel wanted is far greater than the consequences of their actions.

You're like a drug to me. I want you so much and need to have you in my life. I will do anything for you, but you won't do the same for me. I want you so much at any cost. I will do what you ask me to just to be with you. And yet you go away from me to be with who you want to be. I mean, I will give you the world if you would just ask, but you don't. You just walk away and I am sad. So I do what I have to do to keep you in my life, and still you do whatever you like.

I want you like the air that I breathe, but you want me like pulling some weeds…in the hot desert heat. But wait a minute. Hold on! You will fight to keep me won't you?

When you want me you want me, and when you don't you don't. So I sit and wait for you to want me again. And when you take too long, I run to find you, but only to see that you have gone away. Now the chase is on to find you again, only for you to leave me again. I will fight to keep you once again, and then wait, and watch as you leave me again.

I was tired of wondering when, and if, he would ever choose just me. I believed every lie he said, because I was so desperate not to feel any pain. We can really manipulate our own selves to believe what we want in order to feel a certain way. If our minds are strong enough to make us stay in relationships that aren't real, then our minds are strong enough to help us stand up for ourselves! We just have to want it! Well he never chose "only me" and that broke my heart. Now, I am back to pain. This time, however, I did not want to run anymore; this time, I was tired of me. I could not and did not want to run from anyone else again!

Chapter 8

A NEW BEGINNING

I came to realize that my drug use was due to a lack of love ... a love that I wanted and needed, but never had. I knew God loved me unconditionally, but how was I supposed to get back to Him? I was so wrong for using drugs all those years and I was a mess. I felt guilty about not being there for my kids and I wanted a relationship with them more than anything else.

I was searching for love in all the wrong places, but I believe I gave up on love and tried to replace it. It did not work, however, because love kept calling me, it kept urging me to come and find it. I would talk to God and I would pray all the time, but I couldn't really get back to that place and time when I was with my God mom. That was the closest I felt to God...hmmm, maybe that is what I needed, I needed God. Wait a minute, really, didn't He allow all these things to happen to me? I could not trust Him either. Well, God kept calling me and I began to feel his pull stronger and stronger every day.

So I decided to give my life to Christ. That was the beginning of a brand new life. In fact, I would not be writing this book if it were not for the relationship I have with my Father. I love Him so much, but only because He loved me first.

The man I was (falsely) in love with still tried to contact me from time to time and I did the same. But God had other plans for my life. Funny thing is I tried to get back with this man even after he cheated and lied even more, until I had a realization one day. I woke up and told myself, "Sharon, you can believe whatever you want that comes out of this man's mouth or you can look at his behavior patterns and see the truth from there."

The Lies

Everything he said made sense to me only because I wanted to believe him, not because there was any truth to it at all. So I made myself look at the patterns of behavior from the beginning of our relationship to the very end. And to my surprise, nothing had ever really changed. The only thing that really changed was that he got a little better at hiding his mess. Lying became very easy for him, because I believed it. I was equally lying to myself. My own crooked behaviors recognized his warped behaviors and even approved of it on some level. I lived a lie for so long, because I was lying to myself and everyone around me about my drug use. A liar will believe another liar. This was the case with me. Like behaviors have a way of finding themselves in the same arena, whether we realize it or not.

As I look back now, lies were me! I lied about who I was and what I was doing and if anyone ever challenged me on me, I would deny it 'till the death of me. You could not tell me I was smoking crack, because you never saw me, and that was the end of the story. I lied to myself all the time like telling myself that it isn't that bad, or that he had a reason to text the other girl in the middle of the night. I also used my horrible childhood as an excuse. I thought that none of it was my fault, because God should not have let me grow up in that atmosphere. I made myself believe that I wouldn't have ended up the way I did if not for my mom and God. These were all excuses to my bad behavior.

Have we ever really thought and observed the individuals in our lives...the ones we call friends and confidants? Who are these people? Do they resemble us? Do they do things that we absolutely despise? Then ask yourself why. I have a sneaky suspicion that you might find some of you in the people you partner with. I found my "liar" self in that man, but I would not see it for myself at that time. I allowed him to lie to me and even believed his lies, because I was the liar. I have finally come to face the reality of who I really was. This was the beginning of my healing. When I learned to face "me" for who I was, and when I started being true to myself, then I opened the door for change. Therefore, here goes my journey to the real me.

My name is Sharon and I was a drug user, religious alcoholic, promiscuous, and a liar.

BETRAYAL
(Poem)

I can't believe the betrayal you caused me. You want me
to believe that you love me. You will go and do the extraordi-
nary things to ensure that I know you love me, and
then you lie!

You let me down. You make me think that we will have a
good life. You make me believe that everything is going to
work out alright, but now you are caught, and it is all my fault!
I am the bad guy now.

I tell you a thousand times to just let me know if you want
to go, but you say "No, it's you I want" and in a moment of
weakness I believe you, or is it me I believe? I mean what is
wrong with me that I can't see how you are manipulating me?
Is it because I manipulate me? Is that it?

If I could just be honest with me then I could see how dishonest you are being to me, but if I am lying to me I can't see how you are lying to me. So I need to wake up to me before I can even begin to think about waking up to you, is that it?

Oh wow, now I see!

I see that the very things I dislike about you are some of the things that I see in me, and is it that I hate me? I can't see me because I refuse to allow myself the time of day to recognize that my existence even matters because of the hatred I have for me? Do I even allow myself to do the things I do because of the hatred I have for me, or is it for you?

Am I blaming you or should I blame myself for allowing me to hate me? If I hate me, then I will stay far away from me, then I don't have to deal with me. If I hate myself then my very existence is devalued to the lowest form. And why do I hate me?

Is this what I have been taught? Is this my belief system that is embedded into my heart?

Chapter 9

REJECTED!

As I look back over this book, I can still feel the rejection of others, and this feeling shaped my life in a terrible way. I was rejected by my mother and step-father and that drove me to search for acceptance from some of the deepest, darkest places on this earth.

Rejection makes you feel like no one loves you, like you are not good enough and that no matter how hard you try, you will never be good enough to get what or who you want. I lived my life in rejection and fighting to stay in relationships that rejected me. I ran after the very thing that hurt me. I had this tape playing in my head from a child that said, "You will not get any man unless you do whatever he tells you, because you are the darkest. You will have to do whatever people want you to, because no one wants to be around dark people." I had to learn, and am still on a journey of making sure, that these tapes stop playing forever! Although these words don't haunt me anymore, the thoughts of "I am not good enough" try to rise every now and then. "Am I capable of giving and receiving love at all?" is what I thought most of the time. I always came up with the same answer..."No!"

If an individual rejected me, I would do anything in my power to keep them around, and most of the time I didn't even like these individuals. It was just that they didn't want me and I was aiming to please them. I felt as though if I did not give my all, or what others call excellent service; I was not doing what I could to keep what I wanted. And of course, that was unacceptable to me. I had to be wanted and needed. That also became an addiction.

REJECTION CAN BE AN ADDICTION. I was also the main thing that kept me in pain. I lived this pattern of my life for so long that I did not know how to turn off rejection and to be quite honest, I didn't even know that rejection was part of my battle in recovery. All I knew was that I didn't want anyone to leave me or to dislike me, and then once I got them, it didn't matter that I had them until they wanted to leave me. And then I had to fight to keep them! There were times when I believe that I sabotaged the good relationships I had, because they did not reject me. All I knew was what I had been taught and anything different was not accepted in my mind. Even though it may have been good for me, it was different from the way I had been treated, and that was simply not okay.

I would be so heartbroken when people rejected me and that sent me back to drugs and alcohol. That was the chaotic pattern of my life. Toward the end of my addiction, this was the only pattern of my life: I had to have a reason to use and so by creating an atmosphere of pain, I had an excuse to use. Because no one deserved to feel pain, right?

So what do we do with the feelings of rejection? We reject them. If not, we will not recover. We have to start recognizing that we live under and in the confines of rejection.

We are worth more than our negative stinking thinking! We are capable of love and respect and we deserve more than just good enough! We are capable of so much more! We just have to believe.

Chapter 10

WHAT GOD TAUGHT ME

I have discovered so many things along this journey. Other than the ones I have already shared in the previous chapters, I want to share with you the most important lessons I have learned as a result of my pain, hurts, rejection, and addiction.

Forgive and Move On

I brought my past with me and tried to fix it, while I was attempting to heal myself. It never worked. We need to let go of the past first. This requires releasing forgiveness to those who have hurt us. Only then can we begin a new future. Get healed first, and allow God to guide you on the next steps to take.

Love, Lust, or Loss

Oftentimes, we will mistake love for a number of things in which it is not! "Love is not Loss and Love is not Lust." Let me explain the Lust portion first.

The definition of lust is a strong emotional desire for one's body. Most people are in relationships right now based on their emotional connection to their mate's body and how it makes them feel. This is nothing more than another form of addiction. We tell ourselves that we love these individuals and we can't live without them based on pure sexual drive. Love is much more than a sexual and emotional mind trip that allows you to feel wonderful when you need it to. The love that this world knows/portrays is in no comparison to the love that God has for us. It is easy to get lust confused with love if you do not know what true love is. True love comes from above and most of us never had true love portrayed to us in our childhood, so the only form of love we know of is from what we saw and experienced. Most of that portrayal had nothing to do with love. I remember as a child my mom and stepfather used to fight and then go in the room and come out smiling. To me, I downloaded that as a normal relationship.

So, as I grew up, I expected to see this in my relationships and if I did not, then something was wrong. Looking back now, I know that every time I would get a good guy, I couldn't figure out why I couldn't be with him. Well now, I see why. The good guy was not what had been downloaded into my brain. So when I went to search for what I trust (and by trust I mean what I was used to seeing relayed to me repeatedly) in my mind he was not there. This good guy was not a part of anything I knew about, so I immediately rejected it as unknown in my heart and mind. This is why it is so important that we are careful what we allow ourselves and our children to download in our hearts and minds.

Now let me explain the Loss portion of love. Loss is defined by Webster's dictionary as "failure to keep or to continue to have something; the experience of having something taken from you or destroyed." With that being said, Loss is real!

Many individuals cannot stand or even fathom the thought of losing anything. This probably comes from personal loss that has happened to them at some point in their life. So people will fight to the death not to lose anything else. Some men do not like to lose, and the same goes for some women as well. However, men are more competitive than women are. How do we know if their download of Love is Loss?

If they come from a highly competitive parenting lifestyle, then their love language could be one of loss. So they will fight like heck to keep you, but that is not really love; they just don't want to lose anything. Others may come from the mindset of actual loss of someone that was close to them and the very thought of losing anyone else is just too much to handle, so they fight to stay in a relationship that is unhealthy for them. Our brains have a way of alerting our hearts to danger, so if we perceive danger coming, we will do anything to protect ourselves from it. Loss is not love, although many confuse it as such.

We have a way of ensuring that we do not feel pain. Some people use drugs and others use human beings. Either way, this is a pretty unhealthy way to view and perceive love. Being afraid of losing someone or something is just what your mind says it is. Whatever loss is to you, and whatever way you have been taught to deal with loss is how you will deal with it. Viewing loss as detrimental, not an option, and the "I will never let that happen to me" mindsets only set you up for bondage and failure. It will set you up for bondage, because it will keep you attached and seeking after something that could very well be harmful to your mental health.

We must deal with our emotions and feelings, period. We must face whatever we are hiding within ourselves. In other words, those overwhelming feelings of "I refuse to allow myself" must be checked. We should learn to get into the habit of knowing what and why we feel what we feel. What is the motivation behind what we feel? This may take us actually writing down why we feel what we feel and then fact checking those emotions with true reality of the situation. Example, if you are telling your girlfriends or guy friends that the person you are with loves you for real, then why are you checking their phone records? Why are you crying yourself to sleep at night? Why is it okay to push you and shove you? Why is it okay for them to verbally abuse you? And the most important question of all is why do you continue lying to yourself, saying that it will be okay? Bad behaviors must be nipped in the bud. The moment you see them is the moment you need to address them. If you do not, then you only set yourself up for more pain. If you allow a little lie, then rest assured that the big lie is coming around the corner sister!

So then, what is true Love?

My definition of true love comes from the Word of God (1 Corinthians 13:4-8, New International Version).

4Love is patient, love is kind. It does not envy, it does not boast, it is not proud. 5It does not dishonor others, it is not self-seeking, it is not easily angered, it keeps no record of wrongs. 6Love does not delight in evil but rejoices with the truth. 7It always protects, always trusts, always hopes, always perseveres. 8Love never fails.

Now, I want to take some time and deal with some issues that keep us in bondage.

First of all, love is patient, but it does not mean that you patiently wait to be abused or misused by another person. We cannot go on using this portion of Scripture as an excuse to allow others the opportunity to continue to hurt us. We cannot use this as an excuse to stay connected to individuals who mean us no good. We can love from a distance and we must in these cases. We have to be able to know that we are making a conscious decision to choose not to allow anyone to cause us pain. IT IS OUR CHOICE, NOT THEIRS!

Secondly, love does not keep a record of wrongs, but you better make sure that you keep a record of pattern. In other words, if someone's behavior shows a certain pattern, stop trying to make yourself believe that it is not what the proven pattern is. We have to stop manipulating ourselves into believing what we want things to be and to accept people for who they show you they are. Now you can still pray for their change, but you have no say or control over if and when that change will happen. Sometimes distance is good.

Thirdly, Truth is Truth. Do not allow yourself to manipulate the truth of the patterns of another's behaviors. Stop lying to yourself about what it is that you see and have experienced. If an individual is a liar he/she is just that...a liar! Don't make excuses for their behavior.

Fourthly, keep hope alive, yes, but from a distance. We cannot change anyone. Real effective lasting change has to come from within. And if you think you can make someone change by being their personal coach when they are not paying you to do so, then you're working for free. We have to stop telling ourselves that we can change anyone. We cannot do it, only God can, and that individual has to want to change. If they do not want to change their behavior, then we need to stop trying to make them change. One thing I do know is when we tell ourselves we are helping them; this is one of the biggest strongholds I believe exists in our mindsets as humans. Some individuals tell themselves that they are helping people when in all actuality; all they are doing is getting the fix they need.

Chapter 11

PAIN

I found out that through all this pain, I was learning something. I learned that pain comes, and we can let it destroy us if we choose to, or we can learn and grow through it and move in it. Addictions taught me that pain was something that I could not and did not want to feel, but what I have learned is that pain is a part of this life. So, if pain is a part of this life, I cannot afford to allow it to run my life. I had to be able to deal with pain. I could allow myself to feel what I did not want to feel in order to get better. I still had to live in a painful state. This was a concept that I had never known before. All I ever wanted was to feel good and ensure that I was happy. But in order to do this, I had to use.

It is not okay to use drugs, alcohol, sex and/or relationships as a crutch to ensure happiness. I cannot rely on other things to ensure that I will be happy. I had to find true joy and I found that joy in God. As I traveled and am still traveling this road to recovery, I know now that without God I could not have and will not make it. Learning to love and being honest with myself has been a huge challenge for me.

The pain of rejection is another huge hill that I am currently overcoming. I cannot be concerned with others and what they think of me, and my happiness is not based upon whether someone on this earth loves me or not. I have experienced a time in my life where I felt as if no one loved me. I had to live through that pain clean and sober in order to know if I could make it. Replacing one addiction with another is not true recovery; it is just another addiction that you choose not to recognize. If you want to recover fully, you have to be stripped of everything that keeps you thinking you need it in order to be truly happy. Of course, there are stages and steps in this process, but true recovery cannot be reached without going through this process.

Pain must be dealt with severely. It creates holes of devastating proportions when left un-dealt with...holes that break boundaries.

Pain is a part of this life as we know it, but pain does not have to run us. We should begin to look at pain as if we are the driver of the bus. Pain gets on the bus most days, but it is that one thing that does not want to go away. Pain is going to be a constant rider of life, because people come and people go, things come and things will go. Pain comes, but I don't have to like it and I will make sure that you don't stay here longer than you are entitled!

Pain is something that we don't choose to want to have. If we had our way, we would keep it far from us at all times, but it is not something we have control of. It is not something that is within our means to stop all the time, but the matters of the heart we all must go through, and then learn to Thrive!

So, pain comes and it's here, but we must abruptly stop its cheers! Oh, I feel you, I feel you to the core, you hurt; you cry and then beg for more. Realizing that pain is a part of life, do we run from it? Do we hide? Do we embrace it because we realize that pain is a part of life and then learn to live in a painful state of mind? If we accept to live in pain, it only causes more harm.

So we accept pain, we live with pain, we do pain, so we are not thrown off guard, but in all reality, pain is hard. We teach pain to our children, and they do pain too, they think pain is good, their partners are pain, their work and play too.

What we have failed to learn and what we fail to understand is that pain is a part of life, NOT a dwelling place! Pain is real we all know it, it's going to get on the bus and there is nothing we can do about it. However, I believe we can shorten pain's length of stay; we have to get mad at it and want it to go away.

We can't be afraid of it and make it our friend, in order not to get thrown off guard again. We all know the saying "keep your enemies close," well not this one, it won't work. So now that I am the driver of the bus, I am going to tell you when to get off! How about you do what I say do! Your stop is nearing now and you will do what you are told to! I will dictate to pain when it should go, is that plausible, is that so? Can I just tell pain when to go? If it were so easy, we would never need another pill, a doctor, or psychiatry. Is this true reality? Can we give pain its marching orders? Can we tell it to go after it has shown up at the door? I believe we can to a certain degree.

One thing we must not fail to realize is that pain hurts indeed, but how much do we have to take and how much does pain really get to stay? Who we are and who we shall be, how we will live and when to go...For real, I just want pain to end its cruel role!

So I know a place where pain won't be allowed, it's called Heaven, Heaven above. See, the King of Kings and the Lord of Lords will not allow pain to dwell in His holy abode.

So what is the lesson we are to be taught? Pain is pain and it is a part of this life.

What we can do is say to pain that this day, this moment, you have to go away, we can shorten its length of stay most definitely, but we have to find the strength in God and He will show us how to be. God has taught me that I have power from above; I dictate to pain, I tell it where to go, straight to Hell on the quickest road!

So when pain comes, and it will indeed, I will stop at the stop and take it around a block, then I will look back at pain and tell it "this is your stop". Pain looks at me and says, "I will most certainly be back for another ride one day." I tell pain "Yeah, yeah I know you will, but today, I am the driver and you are the rider and this, pain, this is the last stop for you today!

Chapter 12

DISCOVERING YOURSELF

What tapes are playing over and over again in your head? Why are you who you are? Asking yourself these questions will help unlock things for you. Digging deep can be hard on us emotionally, so make sure that you have some support when doing this. If you want change, then you have to do something different; and permanent change requires finding out why you are the way you are in the first place. Taking this journey requires being honest with yourself, if you are not, then this exercise will not help you.

One thing about self-honesty is taking accountability for what you have done in the process of your life. Now you may have learned some bad behaviors and thought processes, but when did you first realize that your behaviors and thoughts were unhealthy to yourself, as well as others? Did you do anything to change, or was changing just too hard? If you just resorted back to your old ways because of familiarity and comfort, then you need to start all over today. Recognizing that the behaviors and thoughts you learned were unhealthy and that you have passed on these unhealthy patterns to others is the next step. Only then can we get down to real change.

The questions below can serve as your guide.

- What were you taught as your value as a child?
- What behaviors were downloaded in you as a child that you still portray?
- What negative downloads need to be replaced?
- How will you start to replace the negative downloads to your mind? (Be honest with yourself. Will you need help replacing them?)
- In what ways do you view yourself as valuable?

Take a deep mental note on how you got to the answers you came up with, where did the answers come from, and why did you come up with the answer? Do any of the answers you came up with hold value to you today? If so, why?

CONCLUSION

My journey of pain and rejection brought me to where I am today. With God's help, I have been able to work with women who are and were just as broken as I was. I worked for two years as a case manager for homeless and addicted individuals. My starting point at this job was all God-led.

I started as a volunteer and then eventually landed a job as shift coordinator, which is basically helping clients with their needs and being a moral support to those who needed it. In two months, my boss Chris promoted me to case manager. I can tell you that God places individuals in your life to help bring out your best potential. This man pushed me and pushed me. We have had some very intense discussions on how things should be and he still listened to me. He was, in fact, my greatest cheer-leader in my adult life! He told me I could do most anything and that I was capable of so much more. I was never the one to plan for the future, because that would require hope, and God forbid one would have hope in anything, but he always talked about forecasting. The thing is, he gave me the opportunity to thrive, and thrive is what I did! A huge thanks to you sir! While I was there, I was able to relate to so many different individuals because of what I had been through personally. I was almost finished with my degree when I started, so I had a full plate while I was working there. But my experience there is what pushed me more into writing this book.

God took a drug-addicted, hopeless, broken me, cleaned me up, and put me in a place where I could share my story with others who were going through what I had been through. I learned how important it was to share my story with others while working there. If we cannot be transparent to help another, then what are we doing here?

My journey of pain was not for no reason. It was to help other individuals. That became so much more evident, as I worked each day with these broken people. I learned that they do not just want some case manager there to tell them what to do and act as though they got it all together. Rather, they want a real life individual who can get on their level of pain. Being able to relate to the pain that others feel is crucial to their recovery.

Knowing that God had this all planned from the beginning really helped me to release the anger I had towards God and to forgive Him as well. Yes, I said forgive God. When I got real honest with myself, I had to admit that I was really angry with God for allowing all the people who I loved to reject me, but in all reality, it was for someone else.

See, I believe that we are placed here to help the next person. And if we are not helping someone else, then what are we really doing? This world can be so self-centered that it is about time we start taking accountability for our actions and non-actions towards one another.

As of the time I am writing the end of this book, I already have my AA in Human Service Management and A Chemical Dependency Trainee Certificate through the state of Washington. I have been given the greatest opportunity to give and receive love from all of my children. This is a dream come true! My children have forgiven me and we even have adult sleep-over's. It is amazing! Talk about making up for lost time. So, from broken to now, I think I am doing just fine. Actually, I am doing wonderful, from the beginning of this book to the end. My life has changed so much for the better and that it is unbelievable! I have some health struggles, but I believe that also has its purpose!

I just want everyone to know that the door to my job shut at an unexpected time in my life, but if it had not, I would not have finished this book in the time that I did. So thank you to those who played a part in that. Thank you God for knowing and seeing what I could not; and for guiding me through this journey of pain called my life.

ABOUT THE AUTHOR

Sharon Blake is a mother of three children and "nana" to four grandchildren. Sharon herself has overcome some major barriers in her life; she has been homeless and is an ex-addict, ex-prostitute and a domestic violence survivor. The person she became originated from her childhood and would require a major overhaul of her thoughts, will, and her emotions. Her desire is to promote hope and healing to those who need hope and healing. Sharon's life would not be her life without the love of her father Jesus Christ; to him she owes more than she can give. This is her way of giving her life away, by being transparent in order to help someone else.

She has an AA degree in Human Service Management, as well as Chemical Dependency Trainee Certificate through the state of Washington. Her work with the homeless/addicted population has inspired her to share her story; this is where she recognized the importance of being transparent in helping others.

The goal for writing this book is to help shed light on why individuals get to some very desolate places in life. Her forecasted programs include creating women's recovery and support groups, as well as opening a women's home to help women get off the streets.

RESOURCES

Your Pain Has Purpose if You Give it a Voice.

VISIT MY WEBSITE TODAY AT

www.mylifechronciles.org

RESOURCES

If you are struggling with drug addiction, alcoholism, domestic abuse, prostitution, thoughts of suicide or any other issue, you can contact me at my website, or the resources below. You are not alone!

Janice Davis Ministries is a Non-Profit 501(c)(3) Charitable Organization outreach ministry bringing hope to the hopeless. Our ministry is transforming the lives of men, women, youth and families through motivation, inspiration, education, spiritual counseling and providing holistic services.

www.janicedavisministries.org

RESOURCES

Rock Paper Scissors (RPS) gives a voice to those who've been silenced from all forms of abuse, low self-esteem, and human trafficking. Our mission is to prevent and heal. (RPS) is creating referral based programs for survivors of all forms of abuse and human trafficking. RPS will provide psychological, medical, and health services along with college advisors and styling teams to help them in their journey. We are also working on forming a hotline to advice victims and potential victims on abuse prevention while providing emotional and physical support. RPS will work hand in hand with individuals to build strong relationships with professionals who, with love, will help these survivors return to a full and vibrant life.

Visit our website today for more information and join a community of people who are healing and taking back their lives.

www.rockpaperscissors2014.webs.com
www.facebook.com/RPS.RockPaperScissors

RESOURCES

I Am Her Voice is a non profit human trafficking organization within the United States. I Am Her Voice speaks for the thousands of women and girls who have gone through the brutality of human trafficking and the thousands who are still trapped and who have no voice. I am her Voice's mission is to eradicate human trafficking amongst girls in the U.S. and be a voice for women and girls who have been domestically assaulted on college campuses. For more information, assistance or rescue services you can go to http://www.iamhervoice.org E:info@iamhervoice.org P:202-810-5951 If you are in danger, call 911. If you are in need of immediate rescue, call 1 (888) 373-7888 National Human Trafficking Resource Center SMS: 233733 (Text "HELP"or "INFO") Hours: 24 hours, 7 days a week The National Domestic Abuse Hotline: 1-800-799-SAFE (7233)

Be Her Voice!

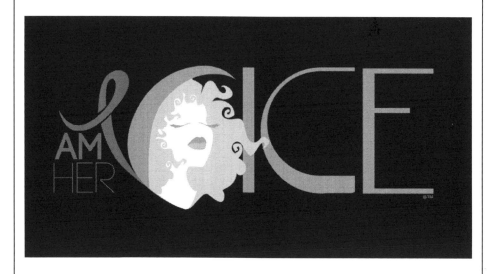

www.facebook.com/IAmHerVoice/timeline

Below is a list of local and national resources available for you. No matter what you are going through, there is a way out and a means of help available to you.

- Nation Coalition Against Domestic Violence http://www.ncadv.org/index.php
- Domestic Shelters http://www.domesticshelters.org
- No More http://www.nomore.org
- The National Domestic Violence Hotline: 1-800-799-SAFE (7233)
- Women's Law http://www.womenslaw.org
- National Institute on Drug Abuse http://www.drugabuse.gov
- SAMHSA http://www.samhsa.gov
- Suicide Prevention Hotline 1-800-273-TALK (8255) TTY:1-800-799-4889 http://www.suicidepreventionlifeline.org
- Alcoholics Anonymous http://www.aa.org
- Breaking Free http://www.breakingfree.net

For bulk orders, or bookstore information, please contact:

Hunter Heart Publishing
4164 Austin Bluffs Parkway
Suite 214
Colorado Springs, Colorado 80918

(719) 472-7900 (253) 906-2160
publisher@hunterheartpublishing.com

www.hunterheartpublishing.com